pocketbooks

Frontispiece: photograph by Guy Moreton, 2002

Football Haiku

sakkaa no haiku

Football Haiku

Alec Finlay
photographs by Guy Moreton

pocketbooks
Morning Star Publications
Polygon
BALTIC
STEC
Tramway

2002

Published by:
pocketbooks
Canongate Venture (5), New Street, Edinburgh, EH8 8BH.

Morning Star Publications
Canongate Venture (5), New Street, Edinburgh, EH8 8BH.

Polygon
22 George Square, Edinburgh, EH8 9LF.

BALTIC: The Centre for Contemporary Art
PO Box 158, Gateshead, NE8 1FG.

Scottish Touring Exhibition Consortium (STEC)
Crawford Arts Centre, 93 North Street, St Andrews, KY16 9AD

Tramway
25 Albert Drive, Glasgow, G41 2PE

Typeset in Minion, Univers and Frutiger.
Typesetting and artworking by Cluny Sheeler.
Design concept by Lucy Richards with Alec Finlay.
Printed and bound by Scotprint, Haddington, East Lothian.

Published with the assistance of grants from the Scottish Arts Council National
Lottery Fund and Highlands and Islands Enterprise (HI Arts).

A CIP record is available from the British Library.

ISBN 0 7486 6309 6

List of Contents

Editor's Acknowledgements

Football Haiku is a collaboration: with Guy Moreton, who photographed the various featured football events, from the first on Cup Final day 2001, to the last at St James Park, in February 2002; with everyone who contributed poems to the anthology and who participated in the football events; and with Zoë Irvine who composed the audio CD. Guy's photographs record a selection of poems – the complete text can be found in 'School Teams' and the 'Spring Catalogue', which also credit the authors. The T-shirts are all for sale.

    Football Haiku appears alongside a companion volume, *Labanotation: the Archie Gemmill Goal*. Project credits appear at the back of the book, listing the participating individuals and organisations. My thanks go to everyone who has been involved in what has been an ambitious and rewarding project. I would particularly like to thank Ken Cockburn, who led the poetry workshops, and the Project Co-ordinator Vicky Hale.

    I also thank the copublishers, in particular BALTIC: The Centre for Contemporary Art, which supported *Football Haiku* and *Labanotation* as part of my artist and publisher residency.

    I also wish to thank the pocketbooks series designer Lucy Richards; Stevie Dale, Peter Kravitz, Joette Thomas, Jane Warrilow and Lesley Young, for their support with fundraising and the realisation of the exhibition; and Paul Hardy for his Japanese translations. Finally, as ever, my thanks go to the staff of pocketbooks past and present, Ken Cockburn, Laura Coxson, Sophy Dale, Jenny Hadfield, Vicky Hale, Alison Humphry, Mark Landells, Benny Robb, and Cluny Sheeler.

Alec Finlay

The Invitation

A new anthology of football haiku will be published for the 2006 World Cup. This is an open invitation to contribute. The form consists of three lines, one word per line. Variations on the form will be considered sympathetically.

Any number of football haiku may be submitted. These may be in any language (if other than English, please provide a translation). Contributions should be typed on a single-sided A4 page, with name and address included, and sent to pocketbooks.

The deadline for contributions is 1 May 2005.

Football Our World

Anywhere. It could be happening anywhere. Some piled jerseys and a ball; a patch of green or an old red brick wall. As kids we used to play lop-sided games between pairs of Scots pine and copper beech. Now it's Sunday kick-abouts on the Meadows. There between paths lined with cherry trees the peoples of the world parade in glossy strips, play around picnics, pass juice round at half-time, sprawl for a quick breather. Even just passing through I love the different rhythms of the games. Asian, African, Indian and Middle-Eastern kids, so graceful and tricky, and the harrumphing directness of the locals. Look down the length of the park, through the avenues of trees, and the football colours stand out against the pink blossom and green grass. It really could be anywhere.

Football Haiku is an anthology of local-universal poetry, an artistic record of a series of football games, a book of photography, and a clothing catalogue complete with order form. It is one of a series of 'participations' that includes *Without Day: proposals for a new Scottish Parliament* (pb 03), and the forthcoming anthologies *wind blown cloud* and *Bynames*, in which 'professional' and 'amateur' artists and writers appear side by side. Readers are encouraged to be writers.

For each participation an invitation is circulated as widely as possible, as a postcard, on the web, in the art press, by word of mouth, and through teaching projects. Football Haiku evolved into a series of school's writing workshops and football events. Most of the photographs were taken at these events. The book also includes 'School Teams', a selection of the best poems by children. The schools also took part in a parallel participation, dancing Archie Gemmill's classic World Cup goal. *Labanotation: the Archie Gemmill Goal* and *Football Haiku* appear as companion volumes. The invitation for *Football Haiku* is reproduced here, and the project will now continue until 2006. You are invited to submit your own football haiku for the next collection.

Football Haiku is published on the occasion of the World Cup in Japan and South Korea – this explains the bow to haiku, another world phenomenon. The range of contributions and the variety of languages echo that global spectacle, but ours is an epic park kick-about featuring poems that are made to be played-in as much as read. There is no reason why such an event should not be repeated in any local park or playing field. The book is also a cheeky alternative to the commercialisation of brand-name football, and all the selected haiku are available as printed T-shirts, which can be ordered from the Catalogue.

The spirit of *Football Haiku* is play, and some of the most inventive poems were written by children. Not surprisingly, a good number of the 5,000 submissions were awful, as the form has a tendency to produce vast quantities of bad puns. Some poems were partisan, but wanting in humour or real bite. Although some of the haiku are inspired by professional football and football writing – the wit of the terraces, slogans, tabloid headlines, zine humour and the 'true fan' phone-in – others are inspired by direct experience of play.

Although the football haiku form is an amusing take on football, poets can also bring over the immersion in the natural world that characterises traditional haiku – so there are versions of the pastoral here, as well as poems which describe our cultural habit of attending to small spherical objects in order to allow ourselves to enjoy some leisure-time in the natural world.

The presentation of football-as-poetry is a quirky thematic conceit for a book, but this is not an anthology of texts. The 'Spring Catalogue' and 'School Teams' sections contain all 342 poems leaving the rest of the book free for the photography.

The art of photography was the perfect idiom for the project. Some of Guy Moreton's shots strike classic football poses – individual portrait, goal celebration, team portrait, huddle – others are concerned with landscape. They portray figures at play in park landscapes, and suggest the poetic and ecstatic moments that occur in the randomly choreographed interactions of children running free.

The photographs are a record, but they transcend the usual narrative of a football match: no-one is keeping score here. They delight in chases and pursuits – what Guy sees, he sees in a flash, frequently running alongside and within the play. The photograph is a moment composed within a moment; the photograph *is* a haiku. They share the characteristics of stillness, turn and play.

Football Haiku extends into an audio CD, *Football Our World*, a collaboration with Zoë Irvine. This includes a newly commissioned work by Simon Patterson, 'Colour Match', featuring the voice of John Kavanagh who reads the football results on Radio Scotland; and an extended composition by Zoë that overlays haiku, found sound elements, and the voices of children, fans and sports personalities. Hearing the Dundonian accent of Jim Spence alongside the soft Korean voice of Ah-Bin Shim is a beautiful meeting of worlds, a universal song made of particulars. The book also features an Away Team of haiku by Tom Leonard (on the audio CD), overseas players (interspersed throughout the book), and the aphoristic 'Connections' of Kurt Johannessen.

The football haiku seems instantly recognisable but it is derived from a ragbag of inspirations – some sporting others literary – many of which I could only call to mind once the final concept had fallen into place. Structurally, the triadic poetic unit of three words displayed on three lines is an unconscious echo of one of the basic plays in football: the interpassing between two players to go past a third. Other influences worth mentioning include Daley Thomson's T-shirt messages at the Olympics, and those footballers all over the world whose T-shirts are emblazoned with dedications, messages and promises, whether to God or their latest girlfriend. The clumsy, DIY typography is a slap in the face of every slick trademarked designer strip and sponsor's logo. Other precedents include the one-word poem, Concrete haiku, and more specifically the work of the poet-monk Dom Sylvester Houédard, who made this wonderful translation of Basho's most famous haiku:

FROG
POND
PLOP

There was Robbie Fowler's T-shirt, 'Support the Liverpool Dockers', which cost him a fine of some thousands of pounds, but endeared him forever to the Kop; the goal celebrations of Ravanelli and every glory-boy who has ever scored a toe-poke down Hackney Marshes; and tabloid-sports headlines, especially those featuring root vegetables. Also, the T-shirts that the artist Rainer Ganhal presented at the Austrian Pavilion at the 1999 Venice Biennale, each bearing the appeal 'Please Teach Me . . .' in one of the many languages that he was learning.

The melange of styles of football haiku that people have invented from the possible combinations of three words has been a delight. For the past year contributions have been arriving by post and e-mail, from Broughty Ferry and Kiel, from Brooklyn and Bearsden – even a flurry from Croatia, where poets heard of the project through the Australian Haiku Society. Poems bounced around the world speaking to common experiences: watching a dreich game in far-away Kantrida is not so very different from spending a night on the forlorn terraces of Almondvale, as the sunshowers pass overhead.

Alec Finlay

for our team

Dear Tilda

Dear Tilda,

Do you remember that chilly afternoon in Edinburgh, years ago now, when we leaned over the wall by the National Galleries, and watched four kids playing football in Princes Street gardens down below. We were almost directly above them, standing in the Gods. It must have been winter as the flags for the putting green had been taken in. They played their game and the city hurried by. No one else stopped.

It was like seeing what the game of football is for the first time: all the palaver that has become attached to it, the fuss of colours and teams and laws all fell away. I remember turning to say to you, *it's a story, that's all*. And so it is. But, however magical the tale, there can only be a few possible outcomes, and just what they are we all know, always.

The team with the ball has a two-to-one advantage. This time it's the kid with the blue jersey who stays in goal. The ball is passed from one attacker to the other, either left or right, so that it passes the single defender. He runs wildly to-and-fro in that mirror space between attacker number one (the tall skinny one) and attacker number two (who is always laughing). Either the kid who is defending guesses right and intercepts the pass – there is only ever one pass – or he doesn't. If he doesn't manage to intervene then a drive is fired in towards the two coat bundles and a goal is scored, or not, and one of two possible endings is written.

The entire game is made up of these two passages of play: first the thing of *the pass*, left or right, the episode of the defender's blind-guess made without ever having the possibility to look round; and the second, the thing of *the shot*, left or right. It doesn't matter what the outcome of each tale is since the score is already something like 18–13 and they are playing first to 30.

In games such as these, unstated laws are extended with each play: you can trip but ankles only; you can play so wide but not that far out; you can tug but not push. With each kick they discover movement; legs seem to become longer; sockets stretch and roll and knees knock; grass stains and grazes appear. A desperate last gasp tackle is missed, and a kid falls, rolls and slumps onto his elbows, all in one motion, leaving go of all care to laugh and give no attention to the other, the attacker, who is about to score. Another time the ball is carried far, far over the imaginary goal line, and dragged all the way round behind the goals, as the two kids canter shoulder to shoulder like a frisky pantomime horse, to re-enter at the other side, and on it goes.

Everything is at the same time real and imagined. The flat surface of the green earth grips onto the ball but when it's up in the air the game swings further towards the imagination. The height of the bar is an extension of the goalie's own height. The play is instantly telescoped in their minds into great sweeping moves: dashes from defence, crunch tackles, rasping drives and incredible fingertip saves. Even from up here we know how to read this dance.

The game isn't played for winning, not really. The longer that it goes on the richer the stories become. Park until dark, the mud-streaked ball ghosted in gloom; a winter game played for the two episodes; played for laughs; and for something more, the blind-guess, and the ending.

Love,

    Eck

FOOTBALL HAIKU

BOUGH SUMMERY LICKS

THE BOYS WATCH

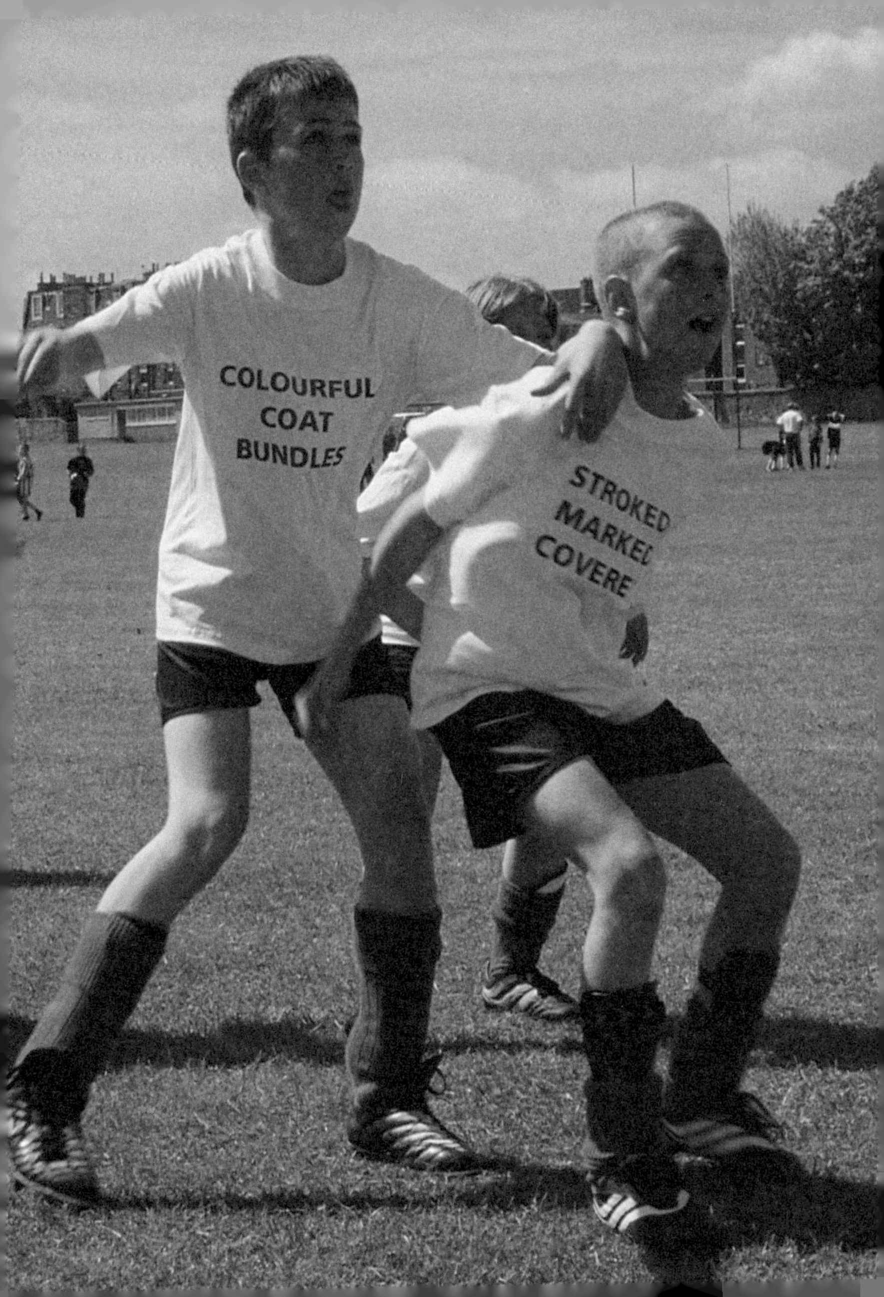
COLOURFUL
COAT
BUNDLES
STROKED

THE GIRLS PLAY

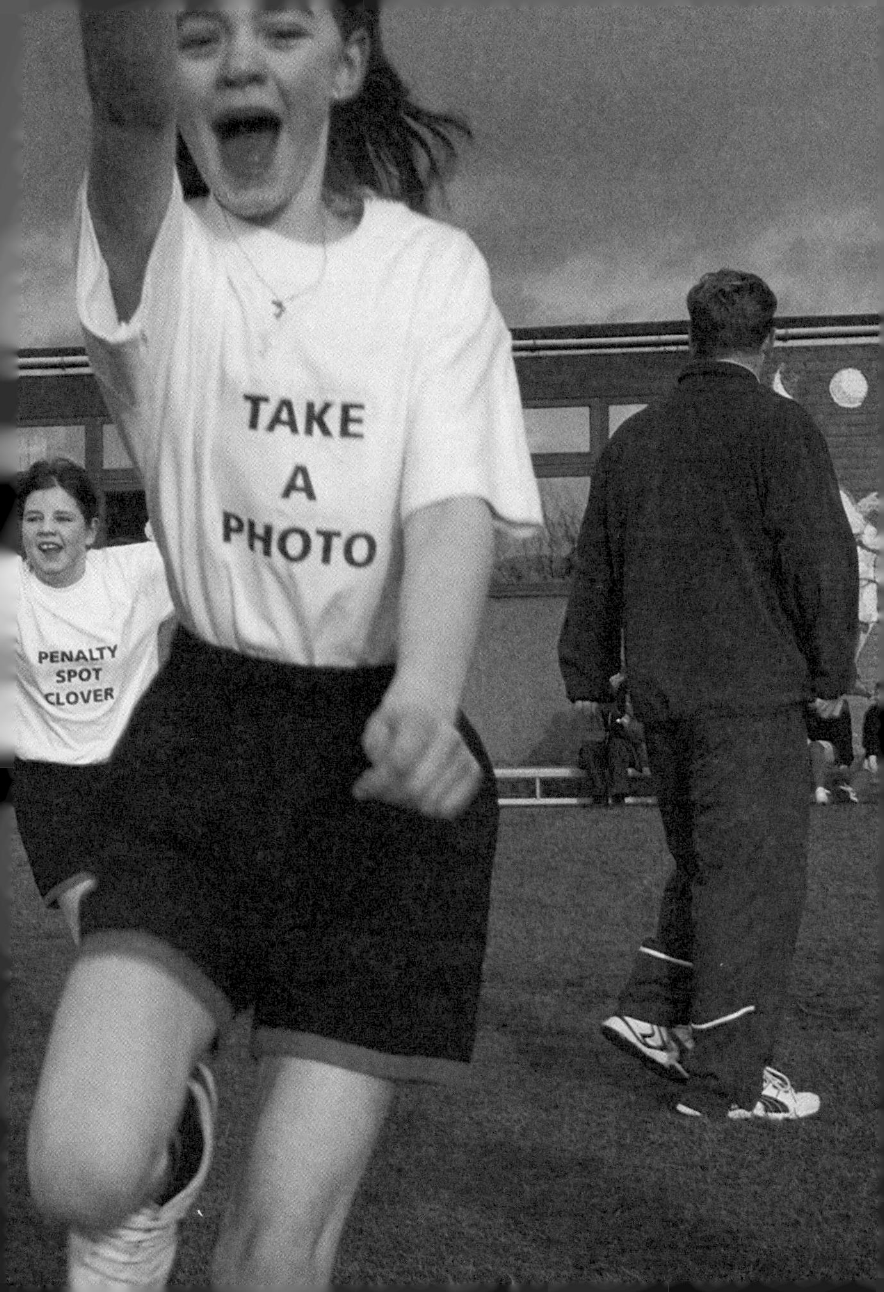
TAKE
A
PHOTO
PENALTY
SPOT
CLOVER

Goooaaalll!
No-one notices
the rain.

HaOwMaEy

Connections

The connection between the problem of keeping the ball on the ground, and a full moon.

The connection between the understanding one has of sophisticated debates at corner kicks, and the moments prior to the epiphany that one has in childhood concerning that whole thing about the stork.

The connection between one's unrealisable dream of being the king dribbler of all time, and one's secret admiration for Scandinavian dance bands.

A World Cup without Scotland is like a pastoral without sheep.

NEWCASTLE

This is how it starts
Kick-off The action Full-time
This is how it ends

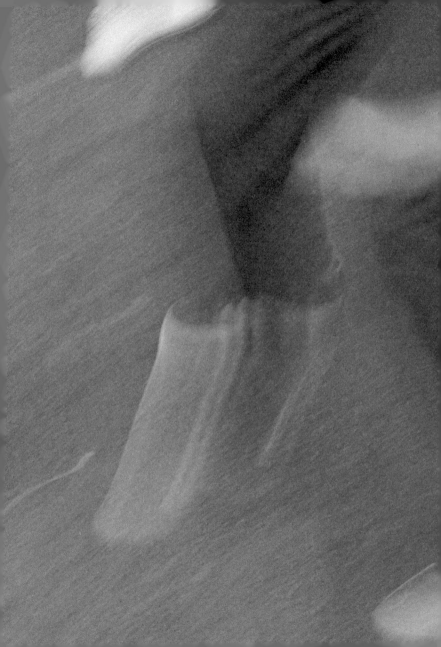

WILD ABSTRACT MOVES

KINDER SPIELT MIT

*Aye, bumface, ye're gaun
in goal! roars this shilpit kid
first time I turn up*

SCHOOL TEAMS

BURNFOOT COMMUNITY SCHOOL

LOCHARBRIGGS PRIMARY SCHOOL

METHILHILL PRIMARY SCHOOL

WYNDFORD PRIMARY SCHOOL

JOHN SPENCE COMMUNITY HIGH SCHOOL

CRAIGMUIR PRIMARY SCHOOL

DONKEYS
LIONS
KINGS

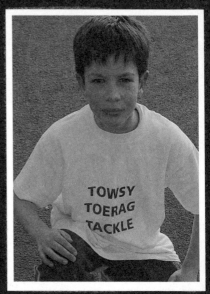

TOWSY
TOERAG
TACKLE

DULL
GOLDEN
GOAL

THE
ONLY
JAY

SEASONS
IN
STRIPS

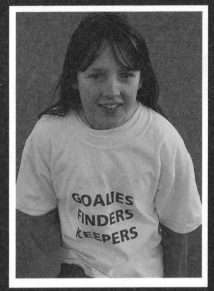

GOALIES
FINDERS
KEEPERS

GUO
PULE
KLINKEKULE

HEY
I'M
OPEN!

Burnfoot Community School

BIG
GRASSY
FIELDS

KIRSTY MITCHELL
001

BLACK
DARK
SKY

KIERAN DIXON
002

MUDDY
DIRTY
HARD

STEVEN HOGG
003

YOUR
TEAM'S
RUBBISH

BEN WATSON
004

HALFTIME
JUICY
ORANGES

ANDREW LOTHIAN
005

BARGE
FALL
HIY!

EMILY ANDERSON
006

ROUGH
RED
OFF

TONI PARR
007

WE
WON
FIRST

AMY JOHNSTON
008

MORE
WASHING
NO!

EMMA KNIGHT
009

Wyndford Primary School

FOOTBALLS
TILL MUM
CALLS

GILLIAN WARD
010

BANGING
GREEN
FENCE

EMMA SAVAGE
011

BALLS
OFF
WALLS

ANDREW GREIG
012

WEE
GUY
RUNNING

STEWART HARRIS
013

AIR
IN YOUR
HAIR

JAIMIE-LEE MEARN
014

FALLING
AND
HOWLING

JAIMIE-LEE MEARN
015

SCORING
AND
YELLING

JAIMIE-LEE MEARN
016

3–1
WE
WON

EMMA KANE
017

ICE-CREAM
BARKING
MAD

COLLETTE DAYER
018

Locharbriggs Primary School

WIND
TREES
BIRDS

SANDY
019

WIND
BLOWING
LEAVES

EILIDH MCROBERT
020

TICTACS
BIRDS
CORNER-FLAG

RICKY DALRYMPLE
021

SUNNY
SUNDAY
STADIUM

RACHEL LESLIE
022

NINETY
MINUTES
TO GO

KIRSTY LAIDLAW
023

MEN
SCREAMING
SCORE

MEGHAN MCGILL
024

GOAL
KEEPER'S
GLOVES

DAVID GOODWIN
025

MAN
DOWN
HURT

GARY PAYNE
026

SHOUTING
SCREAMING
FANATICS

DYLAN IRVING
027

Methilhill Primary School

SQUEAKS
THUDS
ECHOES

KHARIS LIPTON
028

SHINING
SPARKLING
BRIGHT

LAUREN
029

TREES
MAKE
GOALPOSTS

STEVEN MURPHY
030

HUSTLE
BUSTLE
RUSSELL

LEE BRYCE
031

WHISTLING
CHEERING
SINGING

KELLY HANDFORD
032

SKILL
IS
BRILL

LEE BRYCE
033

WIN
FEEL
GOOD

RYAN MATHIESON
034

BOYS
WIN
NOTHING

LEIGH GOSK
035

SWEET
AND
SOUR

NICHOLA BREWSTER
036

Craigmuir Primary School

PLAYGROUND
BENCHES
FLOWERS

MICHAEL HUNTER
037

WINDOW
CLATTER
SWEARING

DANIEL M.
038

HARD
PAINFUL
CONCRETE

CLAIRE BRECHIN
039

SOFT
WET
GRASS

DIANA
040

HEAR
THE
FANS

ASHLEY URQUHART
041

LOUD
CROWD
SINGING

NADINE DALGLIESH
042

HERE!
PASS!
GOAL!

CHRISTINA
043

THE
SINGING
PLAYERS

CALLUM MURRAY
044

WE LOST
THEY WON
SAD

CHRIS A.
045

John Spence Community High School

GO
GEORDIE
GASBAGS

CALLUM WHYTOCK
046

PLAY
WITH
MOVEMENT

PHILLIP CARTER
047

SIDESTEP
GLANCE
SLIDE

GEORGE GILLESPIE
048

PEACOCK
ROBINS
SPARROW

AMANDA FRANGLETON
049

FISH
COSTA
FORTUNE

DAVID CONATY
050

MACKEMS
HACKEM
CRACKEM

KANE YOUNG
051

LASS
KICK
BALL

FAYE MILLER
052

HA
WAY
REF!

PETER STRONACH
053

FLAGS
FLY
HIGH

AMANDA FRANGLETON
054

LOVE
THE
BEE

NOT
NOW
MOM

WOODS
BANKS
FLOWERS

GO-
O-AL

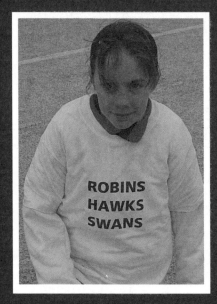

ROBINS
HAWKS
SWANS

ogogogogogogo
oooooooo
ooooooAL

HEGGY
LUGGY
RALPHY

BEAUTIFUL
MISS
SCOTLAND

Beneath the floodlights –
the winger's shadow darts
in four directions

INTERFRENETIC-OTHER-END-MOTIVATED-SPOTTED-BALL-PRODDER

A WIN   AN INEVITABILITY

A LOSS   AN INJUSTICE

a kick-out soaring
way over the centre-line
that's how good I feel

Kantrida!
Sing me a song
of the gulls and the sea

The day passes slowly –
a year from now
the World Cup will be over

SPRING CATALOGUE

poems for parks

FOOT
BALL
HAIKU

CHRISTINE MORRIS
055

BANG
NET
WAH!

BRUCE LEEMING
056

FOOT
BALL
KOAN

MARK GOODWIN
057

KIIRO
KIIRO
AKA

DAVID FAITHFULL
058

EDINBURGH
DRIVES
KAWASAKI

KENNY MUNRO
059

KUNSAN
LOVES
KYLEAKIN

KENNY MUNRO
060

TSUSHIMA
YA
BUTE

KENNY MUNRO
061

POLYSTYRENE
TEA
CEREMONY

JENNY HADFIELD
062

BIG
IN
JAPAN

JOHN MCVEY
063

JOHN MCVEY
064

KEVIN MACNEIL
065

DAVID BAIN
066

DAVID JENKINS
067

KEVIN MACNEIL
068

KEVIN MACNEIL
069

ALEC FINLAY
070

ALEC FINLAY
071

ALEC FINLAY
072

PARKS
KEEPERS
RANGERS

ALEC FINLAY
073

ROLLED
CARPETED
PITCHED

DAVY POLMADIE
074

FEATHERED
WINGED
FLIGHTED

SANDY SALMON
075

STROKED
MARKED
COVERED

SANDY SALMON
076

BENT
SKEWED
TWISTED

DAVY POLMADIE
077

DRILLED
TRAPPED
KILLED

EPIC FILLEY
078

LAYS
CATCHES
SERMONS

ALEC FINLAY
079

WAVES
GESTURES
COMMANDS

DAVY POLMADIE
080

KEEPER
POACHER
FOWLER

SANDY SALMON
081

POTTERS
HATTERS
TROTTERS

RUTH DAVIES
082

GUNNERS
BLADES
HAMMERS

DAVID JENKINS
083

REDS
WHITES
BLUES

DAVID JENKINS
084

SCARLETS
MAROONS
CLARETS

DAVID JENKINS
085

DELL
FOREST
PARK

DAVID JENKINS
086

DEN
PALACE
VILLA

DAVID JENKINS
087

BLUE
FINGERED
CITY

LINDA HENDERSON
088

ROWTH
O'
GREEN

ALEC FINLAY
089

WIND
BLOWN
FLAGS

ALEC FINLAY
090

COLOURFUL
COAT
BUNDLES

DAVY POLMADIE
091

WILD
ABSTRACT
MOVES

JORN EBNER
092

DIRTY
ANKLE
WINGS

ANN VERONICA SMITH
093

THE
BEAUTIFUL
GAME

SANDY SALMON
094

SWAPPING
SWEATY
STRIPS

KEVIN MACNEIL
095

FOOTBALL
BOYS
UGH!

ELLIE REES
096

LUSH
LADS
LEGS

NICOLA SCRIMGEOUR
097

SHORT
SHARP
SOCKS

DREW MILNE
098

INTERNATIONAL
PLAYS
BOYS

MANDY WILKINSON
099

PATRICIA COLLINS
100

EPIC FILLEY
101

ALEC FINLAY
102

SANDY SALMON
103

ZOE IRVINE
104

LORNA J. WAITE
105

LINDA HENDERSON
106

ZOE IRVINE
107

MURDO MACDONALD
108

TAKE
A
PHOTO

ALEC FINLAY
109

MASSED
PIPED
BAND

EPIC FILLEY
110

TOUCH-
LINE
PICNIC

DAVIE POLMADIE
111

PLAY
THE
GAME

JULIE CLARK
112

KNOW
THE
SCORE

JULIE CLARK
113

THROUGH
THE
AIR

DAVY POLMADIE
114

AROUND
THE
GROUND

SANDY SALMON
115

BALL
GHOSTED IN
GLOOM

DAVY POLMADIE
116

TWO
GIRLS
HEADING

DAVY POLMADIE
117

SANDY SALMON
118

ALEC FINLAY
119

ROSS BIRRELL
120

ALEXANDER & SUSAN MARIS
121

EPIC FILLEY
122

SANDY SALMON
123

DAVY POLMADIE
124

TONY KEMPLEN
125

RODDY BUCHANAN
126

STANLEY PELTER
127

JULIE CLARK
128

ANDREW GARDINER
129

TOM BRYAN
130

LAURA COXSON
131

RUARI CONNOR
132

LAURA COXSON
133

JULIE CLARK
134

PHILLIP BEECH
135

NIFTY
PASS
BACK

JAMES MCGONIGAL
136

CROSS
COME
SHOT

TOM HOWARD
137

ACE
KNEE
SLIDE

ELSPETH MURRAY
138

GRASS
BLAZE
GRAZE

DAVY POLMADIE
139

USE
YER
HEID

CLUNY SHEELER
140

HEID
THE
BAW

IRENE BROWN
141

IT'S
SHOOTIE
IN

JOHN MCVEY
142

PICK
THAT
OOT

JIM PATERSON
143

YUR
GAAN
DOON!

TOM BRYAN
144

SEASON
OF
MISSES

DAVID PETTS
145

THE
SEASON
SWEETENS

KEN COCKBURN
146

SPRING
OFFSIDE
TRAP

DAVID A. H. JOHNSTON
147

THE
FIRST
BUDS

DAVY POLMADIE
148

NEW
DEW
SPARKLE

EPIC FILLEY
149

BOUGH
SUMMERY
LICKS

JAMES MCGONIGAL
150

FLIMSY
DAISY

ALEC FINLAY
151

PENALTY
SPOT
CLOVER

DAVID COBB
152

BECKS
FLOWERS
BEST

KEN COCKBURN
153

SUNNY
MEADOWS
ARC

ELSPETH MURRAY
154

SPIDER
WASP
SWIFT

KEN COCKBURN
155

WASP
TRANSPARENT
COURSE

JAMES MCGONICAL
156

GREAT
NORTHERN
DIVER

COLIN DUNNING
157

SWIFT
WING
III

SANDY SALMON
158

SUMMERBEE
STINGS
HOSTS

PHILIP BEECH
159

BOWER
BRAMBLE
OAKES

DAVID PREECE
160

BERRY
BRAMBLE
CHERRY

CLUNY SHEELER
161

SUNSHOWERS
OVER
ALMONDVALE

BILLY WATT
162

BIRRING
BREEZY
DARKER

JAMES MCGONIGAL
163

SEASONS
IN
STRIPS

ZOE IRVINE
164

SMELLS
LIKE
RAIN

SANDY SALMON
165

STUDS
POCKING
HAIL

JENNY HADFIELD
166

SEASONS
ROLL
AROUND

ALEC FINLAY
167

OUR
WINTER
GAME

BILL GRIFFITHS
168

HALFPENNY
HOWLING
SWELL

STUART BENNETT
169

FLOODLIT
WINTER
NIGHT

SEAN WILLIAMS
170

WHYTE
WINTERS
WOODS

DAVID PREECE
171

GRASP
THE
NETTLE

DAVID JENKINS
172

CAP
OF
THORNS

JAMES MCGONIGAL
173

CUP
OF
THISTLES

JAMES MCGONIGAL
174

FLOWERLESS
FOOTBALL
FIELD

STANLEY PELTER
175

WEATHER
THE
STORM

DAVID JENKINS
176

PARK
UNTIL
DARK

ALEC FINLAY
177

THE
BACK
END

CAITLIN DESILVEY
178

VALE
OF
LETHEN

SANDY SALMON
179

SILENCE
IN THE
DELL

ALEC FINLAY
180

WOODS
BANKS
FLOWERS

ALEC FINLAY
181

ROBINS
HAWKS
SWANS

DAVID JENKINS
182

CYRIL
SWAN
SWEEPER

GEOFF SAWERS
183

CANARIES
SEAGULLS
MAGPIES

DAVID JENKINS
184

SEAGULL
TRAWLER
SARDINE

GEOFF SAWERS
185

THE
ONLY
JAY

DONALD URQUHART
186

BARK
UNTIL
SHARK

ARNE RAUTENBERG
187

WOLVES
TERRIERS
RAMS

DAVID JENKINS
188

DONKEYS
LIONS
KINGS

ALEC FINLAY
189

EPIC FILLEY
190

EPIC FILLEY
191

ALAN GILBERT
192

A.RAWLINGS
193

A.RAWLINGS
194

GERRY LOOSE
195

SANDY SALMON
196

ROB TUFNELL
197

ROB TUFNELL
198

PHILIP BEECH
199

THOMAS A. CLARK
200

ALISTAIR JACKSON
201

DAVID PREECE
202

DAVID JENKINS
203

DAVID JENKINS
204

ALASTAIR JACKSON
205

JONATHAN MONK
206

DAVID A. H. JOHNSTONE
207

THAT
GEMMILL
GOAL!

JAMES P. SPENCE
208

GEMMILL'S
GOAL
AGAIN

JAMES P. SPENCE
209

VILLAGE
RADIO
GOAL

ELSPETH MURRAY
210

VERY
OWN
GOAL

DANI HALL
211

DULL
GOLDEN
GOAL

RODDY BUCHANAN
212

OVERSEAS
TEXT
GOAL

ELSPETH MURRAY
213

ONE
MILLION
(NETTO)

KEN COCKBURN
214

PLOP
GOAL
FLOP

PETER FOLEN
215

FOOT
BALL.
NET

RICHARD DEACON
216

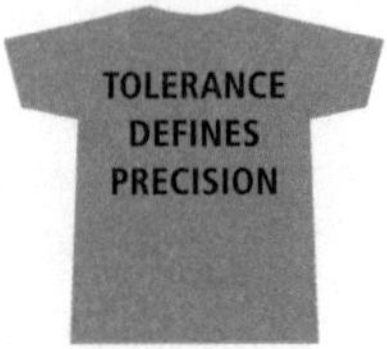

TOLERANCE
DEFINES
PRECISION

DAVID CONNEARN
217

SKILLS
OVERCOME
ENTHUSIASM

LESLIE CARTER
218

POSSESSION
IS
EVERYTHING

IRENE BROWN
219

SITUATION
RATHER
DESPERATE

CHARLES MCCARTHY
220

PERSISTENT
UNWANTED
THOUGHTS

ALEC FINLAY
221

LAMENTABLE
FOUL
FEUD

WATTS PILGRIMM
222

REFEREE
LOOKS
AWAY

STANLEY PELTER
223

SPONSORS
INSIST
PINK

GEOFF SAWERS
224

ATTRACTIVE
NET
CURTAINS

HEATHER WASTIE
225

**RETIRED
MIDFIELD
GENERAL**

IAN MARTIN
226

**PARTICK
THISTLE
NIL**

DAVY POLMADIE
227

**BETWEEN
SWEATERS
THE WINNER!**

DYLAN PUGH
228

**GONNAE
NO
MISS**

SANDY SALMON
229

**PASS
BALLBOY
FLOATER**

TELFER STOKES
230

**GIFTED
UTILITY
SEASONED**

STEPHEN MCCABE
231

**HYDRA
HEIDS
IN**

ANDREW MCNEIL
232

**STRIKING
WINGED
HYDRA**

JENNY HADFIELD
233

**GODS
MEN
MONSTERS**

JENNY HADFIELD
234

ALEC FINLAY
235

DANI HALL
236

STANLEY PARK
237

ALEC FINLAY
238

DAVID PREECE
239

FIONA RIGG
240

DAVY POLMADIE
241

DOUGLAS ROBERTSON
242

ELSPETH MURRAY
243

GORDON YOUNG
244

BASIM FARID
245

GREG DAWSON ALLEN
246

DAVY POLMADIE
247

ALEC FINLAY
248

KEN COCKBURN
249

RODDY BUCHANAN
250

GRAHAM FAGEN
251

BILL GRIFFITHS
252

STAIN
STRIP
STROP

ELSPETH MURRAY
253

SCREEN
CROPS
SCOPE

ELSPETH MURRAY
254

LOOK
AWAY
NOW

EDDIE GIBBONS
255

SUBSEQUENT
PROGRAMS
DELAYED

TONY KEMPLEN
256

SPORTSNIGHT
WITH
COLEMAN

IAIN CRICHTON SMITH
257

SLEEPING
THROUGH
GOALS

SANDY SALMON
258

NOT
NOW
MOM

MATIAS IRRABADAL
259

IT'S
MA
BA

JIM PATERSON
260

PALE
WAN
WUN

ALEC FINLAY
261

WOT'S
YAWR
TAYME?!

BRIAN KIM STEFANS
262

FOOTBALL?
PLAY
QUIDDITCH!

DARREN WERSHLER-HENRY
263

CALL
IT
SOCCER

CHARLES BERNSTEIN
264

POETRY
IN
MOTION

VICKY HALE
265

BLUE
BINOS
BULLY WEE

KEN COCKBURN
266

LITTLE
RED
BOOK

KEN COCKBURN
267

BE
MY
READER

ALEC FINLAY
268

SPRING
WASH
DAY

DAVY POLMADIE
269

MUD
PATCHED
PITCH

SANDY SALMON
270

HEGGY
LUGGY
RALPHY

GAVIN HOWITT
271

MAN
ON,
HAMMY!

DAVID A. H. JOHNSTONE
272

HAMMY!
MAN!
ON!

DAVID A .H. JOHNSTONE
273

BAWHEAD
TUMSHY
CLOWN

ANETTE GILROY
274

PEUK
PAPPLE
PAVILLE

ALEXANDER HUTCHISON
275

COCCHI
OCCHI
TROCCHI

ALEXANDER HUTCHISON
276

DERRY
DAN
DANTE

ALEXANDER HUTCHISON
277

SWIZZELT
SWYVIT
SWANNY

ALEXANDER HUTCHISON
278

BEE
BAW
BOBBITY

ALEXANDER HUTCHISON
279

DONKEY
RAZOR
BUTCH

MILES CHAMPION/TIM ATKINS
280

CHOPPER
SNIFFER
PSYCHO

MILES CHAMPION/TIM ATKINS
281

RADISH
EVIL
CUPTIE

STEPHEN BURY
282

RADEBE
RADEBE
SINGH

LLOYD ROBSON
283

WANCHOPE
SAVAGE
DICKOV

DAVID PREECE
284

HUSSEY
CLISAT
AMANKWAAH

LLOYD ROBSON
285

MERCURIAL
JINKY
JAWS

PAUL DIGNAN
286

BALDE
BAD
DAY

SANDY SALMON
287

AWAYYE
GOYA
MUGYE

JIM PATERSON
288

STEIN-
WAY
BEST

TOM MURRAY
289

SAINT
CLEARS
STALWART

PAUL DIGNAN
290

SILVER
LINING
PATALINEN

BRENDAN JOHNSTONE
291

GARY
HUME'S
TEAM

EPIC FILLEY
292

SOCRATES
OUT-THINKS
DEFENCE

GEOFF SANDERS
293

MIS-
EN-
SCENE

SANDY SALMON
294

PIER
PAOLO
PASOLINI

ALEC FINLAY
295

ROMA
AMOR
ROSA

ROSE FRAIN
296

TORA
FORZA
TORA

DOUGLAS GORDON
297

FUCHS KUNTZ SCHEIDT

HARRY GILONIS
298

DRUCK LUFT MASCHEN

ARNE RAUTENBERG
299

SUSTAINED PRESSURE NETS

tr. KEN COCKBURN
300

MUCKLE-HERTIT SMILING AWEYS

ANDREW MCNEIL
301

KINDER SPIELT MIT

INGRID LEES
302

CHILDREN PLAY WITH US

tr. KEN COCKBURN
303

GRING ABE U SECKLE

FRANZISKA FURTER
304

HEAD DOWN & RUN

tr. FRANZISKA FURTER
305

GUO PULE KLINKEKULE

C EVELIO
306

BORIJOV BUKVA
307

tr. BORIJOV BUKVA
308

SEAN WILLIAMS
309

INGRID LEES
310

tr. KEN COCKBURN
311

DAVY POLMADIE
312

SUHAYL SAADI
313

INGRID LEES
314

tr. KEN COCKBURN
315

KATIE WILLATS
316

ROBERT ALAN JAMIESON
317

ROBERT ALAN JAMIESON
318

JORN EBNER
319

JORN EBNER
320

JORN EBNER
321

ZOE IRVINE
322

IAN HAMILTON FINLAY
323

EPIC FILLEY
324

TOM BRYAN
325

MARION COUTTS
326

HARRY GILONIS
327

KEVIN MACNEIL
328

RONA CAMPBELL
329

BRYAN BIGGS
330

MALCOLM MCCANDLESS
331

MALCOLM MCCANDLESS
332

GREG DAWSON ALLEN
333

LAWNMAN'S
COBALT
MAGIC

KEN SUTHERLAND
334

TREPAN
NUPTIAL
MISCUE

STEPHEN BURY
335

WEASLY
DUDDERS
VERNON

MAX HUTCHISON
336

NOBLE
BATTY
LAMA

HARRY GILONIS
337

DIRTY
THIRTY
FLIRTY

MAX HUTCHISON
338

DANCER
DANCER
DANCER

BRIAN SPEEDIE
339

TOWSY
TOERAG
TACKLE

LORNA J. WAITE
340

I
LOVE
YOU

ALISTAIR TUXWORTH
341

BIRTH
FOOTBALL
DEATH

HOWARD GRANVILLE
342

Whether it's for a kick-about in the park, a day at the beach, or watching those big World Cup matches, Football Haiku T-shirts are ideal casual wear for a Summer full of sport and fun.

ORDER FORM

T-shirts available in Adult or Child sizes. Printed on high quality white cotton. Priced £12.00 (10% off for orders of 3 or more shirts).

CODE	ADULT (M/L)	CHILD (S)

TOTAL NO. OF T-SHIRTS .... @ £12.00   ....

P & P (15%)   ....

PLUS VAT (17.5%) ON ADULT T-SHIRTS   ....

TOTAL COST   ....

NAME   ....

ADDRESS   ....

....

POST/ZIP CODE   ....

COUNTRY   ....

pocketbooks, Canongate Venture (5), New St, Edinburgh, EH8 8BH. Cheques payable to pocketbooks Ltd. Credit card facilities are not available.

PLEASE NOTE ALL T-SHIRTS ARE BLACK TEXT ON WHITE FABRIC

Note on the Text

Featured poems by (in order of appearance): 'Bough Summery Licks', Alec Finlay; 'The Boys Watch', Epic Filley; 'The Girls Play', Alec Finlay; 'Goooaaalll!', Dragan J. Ristic; 'Smells Like Rain', Sandy Salmon; 'HaOwMaEy', David Bellingham; 'Connections' (extracts), Kurt Johannessen, translated from the Norwegian by the author; 'A World Cup', Ian Hamilton Finlay; 'This is how it starts', René Schoemakers, translated from the German by Ken Cockburn; 'Wild Abstract Moves', Alec Finlay; 'Kinder Spielt Mit', Ingrid Lees; 'Aye, bumface', Arne Rautenberg, translated from the German by Ken Cockburn; 'Beneath the floodlights', Matthew Paul; 'Interfrenetic', Gael Turnbull; 'A Win/A Loss', David Bellingham; 'A kick-out', Arne Rautenberg, translated from the German by Ken Cockburn; 'Kantrida!', Borivoj Bukva; 'The day passes slowly', Alec Finlay.

Football Haiku Project Acknowledgements

Thanks are due to the following for their participation in a truly inspiring project.

HOME TEAM: Ken Cockburn, Stevie Dale, Sophy Dale, Alec Finlay, Paul Hardy, Zoë Irvine, Mark Landells, Guy Moreton, Benny Robb, Cluny Sheeler, Joette Thomas, Jane Warrilow and Lesley Young.

AWAY TEAM: 26.05.01 Bruntsfield Primary School, Edinburgh; James Gillespie Primary School, Edinburgh; Dean Park Primary School, Edinburgh; Boroughmuir Primary School, Edinburgh; Granton Primary School, Edinburgh; Towerbank Primary School, Edinburgh; Royal High Primary School, Edinburgh, and Stuart Rafferty, SFA Football Development Officer. **19.11.01 & 21.01.02** Primary 5/6 & 6 pupils at Burnfoot Community School, Hawick; Assistant Head Mrs Hill; teacher Ms Scott; and Dougie Anderson, SFA Football Development Officer. **23.11.01 & 23.01.02** Primary 5 pupils at Wyndford Primary School, Glasgow, Acting Head Teacher Ms Taylor; teachers Ms Black and Ms Carson; Primary 6 pupils from Pinewood Primary School, and teacher Ms Fraser; Andrew Gilcrest, John Brown and Frank Clement SFA Football Development Officers. **27.11.01 & 22.01.02** Primary 6 pupils at Locharbriggs Primary School, Dumfries; Head Teacher Mr Docherty; and teachers Mrs Mechan and Mrs Farmer. **04.12.01 & 25.01.02** Primary 5, 6 and 7 pupils at Methilhill Primary School, Fife; Head Teacher Mr Small, teachers Ms Donaldson and Mr Williamson; and football representative Alex Easton. **21.01.02 & 24.01.02** Primary 5/6 pupils at Craigmuir Primary School, Edinburgh; Head Teacher Mr French and Ms Reith. **05.02.02 & 01.03.02** Year 7, 8 and 9 pupils, Head Teacher Mr Davison, teachers Mr Gillespie, Ms Shepherd, Mr Graham and Mr Ross at John Spence Community High School, North Shields; Newcastle United Football Club, and David Saxon Senior Marketing Executive at St James Park; Roger Tames and Tyne Tees Television. With thanks to Emma Thomas, Sophie Thomson, Sarah Hudspeth, Vicki Lewis and Sune Nordgren and the rest of the team at BALTIC: The Centre for Contemporary Art. Participating members of STEC, The Scottish Touring Exhibitions Consortium: Diana Sykes and the Crawford Arts Centre, St Andrews; Dawn Henderby Dumfries & Galloway Council and Gracefield Arts Centre,

Dumfries; Elizabeth Hume, Scottish Borders Council and Hawick Museum; Cathy Shankland, Highland Council; Alexia Holt, Glasgow City Council and Tramway; Tracy Morgan and Martin Ayres, North Edinburgh Arts; and the Scottish Poetry Library; and the City Art Centre, Edinburgh; Andy Howitt at Scottish Youth Dance, Edinburgh; and Robin Gillanders.

Vicky Hale
Co-ordinator

Touring Exhibition
Hawick Museum, Scottish Borders: 2–23 May 2002
Tramway, Glasgow: 19 –23 June 2002
BALTIC: The Centre for Contemporary Arts, Gateshead: July 2002
Crawford Arts Centre, St Andrews: 30 Aug –20 Oct 2002
Gracefield Arts Centre, Dumfries: 26 Oct–23 Nov 2002
Swanson Gallery, Thurso: January 2003
North Edinburgh Arts: February 2003

Morning Star Publications   Polygon   Scottish Poetry Library

Football Our World

An Aeolus CD

1. The Miracle of Mendoza – Zoë Irvine (2:07)
2. Football Haiku – Zoë Irvine (7:41)
3. Colour Match – Simon Patterson (7.35)
4. Replay – Zoë Irvine (1:04)

Track 1. Archie MacPherson's commentary of Scotland v Holland in the 1978 World Cup in Argentina © Archie MacPherson.

Track 2. Voices in order of appearance: Croatian footballers, Primary 5/6 pupils from Craigmuir Primary School, Jim Spence, Johnny Daniel, players from Newport Amateur Football Club, Ah-Bin Shim, Rob Maclean, Richard Gordon and Dougie Donnelly. Football haiku © the authors (see 'Spring Catalogue'); also including four haiku by Tom Leonard read by Jim Spence.

Track 3. Voice: John Kavanagh.

Track 4. Archie MacPherson's and David Coleman's commentaries of Scotland v Holland in the 1978 World Cup in Argentina © Archie MacPherson and © David Coleman.

Tracks 1,2 & 4 composed by Zoë Irvine; tracks 1 & 4 originally conceived by Andy Howitt, track 2 conceived by Alec Finlay © 2002. Track 3 by Simon Patterson © 2000, commissioned by pocketbooks.

The text of 'Colour Match' comprises the names of all the teams in the Scottish Football League past and present, combined with Pantone colour reference numbers (the international colour standard used by designers and printers).

Acknowledgements

This work was possible due to Alec Finlay's generous collaborative spirit and the enthusiasm that pocketbooks have had for the audio element of this project.

Special thanks go to Jim Spence for his time, effort and voice; to Ken Cockburn and Alec Finlay who brought the poems alive; to Tony Conetta for taking me to Celtic v Rangers; to the pupils of Craigmuir Primary School, Edinburgh, who made such great recordings. Thanks also to Dougie Donnelly, Rob Maclean and Richard Gordon at the BBC in Glasgow who took time out of their busy schedules; Andy Howitt and Annika Joy at Scottish Youth Dance; Helen O' Hanlon at dancebase; Julia Hamilton at BBC Sport, (Glasgow); Jim Preacher BBC Contracts, (Glasgow); Selena Jones at BBC Archives, (Glasgow); Edward Champion at BBC Sport, (London); David Coleman and Geoffrey Irvine; Elaine Howie PR; Ah-Bin Shim at the School of Television & Imaging, Duncan of Jordanstone College of Art, Dundee; Simon Patterson for 'Colour Match'; and Gerald Straub for listening ears.

Produced by Aeolus.

Manufactured by Key Productions, London.

Zoë Irvine
Aeolus

pocketbooks

01 **GREEN WATERS**
an anthology of Boats & Voyages
ISBN 0 9527669 4 9; 96pp, colour illustrations, out of print.

02 **ATOMS OF DELIGHT**
an anthology of Scottish haiku and short poems
ISBN 0 7486 6275 8; paperback, 208pp, £7.99

03 **LOVE FOR LOVE**
an anthology of Love Poems
ISBN 0 7486 6276 6; paperback, 200pp, £7.99

04 **WITHOUT DAY**
proposals for a new Scottish Parliament
ISBN 0 7486 6277 4; paperback, 184pp, with audio CD, £7.99 (incl. VAT)

05 **WISH I WAS HERE**
a Scottish multicultural anthology
ISBN 0 7486 6281 2; paperback, 208pp, with audio CD, £7.99 (incl. VAT)

06 **WILD LIFE**
Hamish Fulton
ISBN 0 7486 6282 0; paperback, 208pp, with audio CD, £7.99 (incl. VAT)

07 **GRIP**
David Shrigley
ISBN 0 7486 6238 9; paperback, 208pp, £7.99

08 **DISTANCE & PROXIMITY**
Thomas A. Clark & Olwen Shone
ISBN 0 7486 6288 X; paperback, 128pp, £7.99